THE EASY PIANO COLLECTION
CHOPIN
GOLD

Published by:
Chester Music Limited,
14-15 Berners Street, London W1T 3LJ, UK.

Exclusive Distributors:
Hal Leonard
7777 West Bluemound Road
Milwaukee, WI 53213
Email: info@halleonard.com

Hal Leonard Europe Limited
42 Wigmore Street
Marylebone, London, W1U 2RN
Email: info@halleonardeurope.com

Hal Leonard Australia Pty. Ltd.
4 Lentara Court
Cheltenham, Victoria, 3192 Australia
Email: info@halleonard.com.au

Order No. CH78639
ISBN 978-1-78038-282-1
This book © Copyright 2014 by Chester Music.

Previously available as book only CH72314

Edited by Jessica Williams.
Arranging and engraving supplied by Camden Music.
Original cover design by the Design Corporation.
CD Project Manager: Ruth Power.
CD recorded and produced by Mutual Chord Studio, Guangzhou, China.

CD manufactured and book printed in the EU.

www.halleonard.com

CHESTER MUSIC

Ballade No.1 in G minor, Op.23
Page 5

Barcarolle, Op.60
Page 6

Berceuse, Op.57
Page 8

Cantabile in B♭ major
Page 64

Chorale from Nocturne, Op.37, No.1
Page 10

Étude No.3, Op.10
Page 12

'Fantaisie' Impromtu, Op.66, No.4
Page 14

'Funeral March' from Sonata No.2, Op.35
Page 16

Largo in E♭ major, Op. Posth.
Page 18

Mazurka, Op.7, No.5
Page 22

Mazurka, Op.67, No.2
Page 26

Mazurka, Op.68, No.2
Page 19

Nocturne in E♭ major, Op.9, No.2
Page 23

Nocturne in G minor, Op.15, No.3
Page 30

Piano Concerto No.1, Op.11 (2nd movement: Romance)
Page 32

Polonaise, Op.53
Page 38

Polonaise in A major 'Militaire', Op.40, No.1
Page 36

Prélude in A major 'The Polish Dance', Op.28, No.7
Page 40

Prélude in B♭ major 'Sunday', Op.28, No.21
Page 42

Prélude in C minor 'Funeral March', Op.28, No.20
Page 41

Prélude in D♭ major 'Raindrop', Op.28, No.15
Page 46

Prélude in E minor 'Suffocation', Op.28, No.4
Page 48

Sonata No.1 in C minor, Op.4 (2nd movement: Menuetto and Trio)
Page 50

Waltz in A minor 'Brillante', Op.34, No.2
Page 55

Waltz in A♭ major 'Farewell' (Posthumous), Op.69, No.1
Page 60

Waltz in D♭ major 'Minute', Op.64, No.1
Page 61

Frédéric Chopin

Born in Poland in 1810, Frédéric Chopin was the son of a French émigré father and a cultured Polish mother. Displaying an early talent for the piano, he began his studies at the Polish Conservatory in 1826. In 1829 he made a concert tour, and while he was well received in Berlin and Vienna, the greatest acclaim came in his native Warsaw, where his use of Polish folk melodies and rhythms was particularly appreciated.

As a youngster of 19, Chopin was inspired to compose two *piano concertos* by his love for a singing student, Konstancja Gładkowska. The 'singing' quality of the piano parts is apparent throughout these works and particularly in the lyrical slow movements. The *Romance* from *Piano Concerto No.1 in E minor Op.11* is included in this album. This melodic style is central to Chopin's view of composition.

Chopin settled permanently in Paris in 1831. He found patrons and became a sought-after performer and teacher in high society, where his good looks and impeccable social graces aided his popularity. Two extremes of piano playing and composition emerged at this time: one, championed by Franz Liszt, celebrated flamboyant showmanship and brilliant technical display, the other, represented by Chopin, had its roots in the private drawing room. Chopin composed intimate miniatures which, although requiring a flawless technique and sensitive colouring of the music, were not written to impress, but to express sentiments in an elegant manner.

The piano was the supreme Romantic instrument, reshaped, enlarged, and mechanically improved. Chopin exploited the instrument's new potential, devoting his entire composition career to it. His chromatic harmonies and remote modulations stretched the known harmonic language and he varied his treatment immensely, delaying or extending passages, introducing a greater complexity in the return of a theme, or adding a brilliant 'coda'.

His smaller-scale works, the études, préludes, nocturnes, waltzes, impromptus and mazurkas, were probably written for teaching purposes, particularly the 27 études. These continued a tradition of pieces that used one musical idea to highlight a particular aspect of piano technique. Chopin transformed the étude from a mere teaching aid to a highly significant musical genre. Included in this book is the *Étude in E Major Op.10, No.3*. Chopin's 24 préludes follow Bach's example of writing a set of pieces in every key. The préludes in this album include the famous *'Raindrop' Prélude*, in which the melody is underpinned throughout by a repeated G (originally A flat), suggesting the constant sound of rain.

Perhaps the most evocative of Chopin's smaller forms are the nocturnes. Beautiful melodies are accompanied by delicate, often arpeggiated left-hand textures. Chopin was not the inventor of this form—an earlier Irish composer, John Field, first used the term 'nocturne' to describe a similar style of piece, but Chopin made it his own. The use of 'rubato' to create flexibility within the melody is very important to the effective performance of the nocturnes. Chopin described this technique as a 'pushing forward' or 'holding back' of the right-hand melody while the left hand always plays in strict time. Two nocturnes are included in this album, including the famous *Nocturne in E flat major* with its beautiful, haunting melody.

The mazurka, the polonaise and the waltz are all dance-forms. The triple-time mazurka, a Polish folkdance, was a favourite of Chopin's and he composed 31, three of which are included in this album. These peculiarly Polish melodies are characterised by the strong accent on the second or third beat. The polonaise is also a Polish folkdance, full of heroic spirit. Chopin's 20 waltzes are short, brilliant pieces. This book includes the notorious *'Minute Waltz'*, so called because, if taken at an extreme tempo, it can be played in one minute flat!

Chopin wrote his larger-scale works such as the scherzos, ballades and sonatas for his salon recitals. The Romantic sonata lost the formal structure which characterised Classical sonatas as composers experimented with form. Included here is the famous *Marche Funèbre (Funeral March)* from the *Second Sonata*, as well as the *Minuet and Trio* from the *Sonata in C minor*. These experiments with form resulted in pieces like the *Ballade in G Minor Op.23* which have a strong sense of drama and narrative drive.

In 1834 Chopin composed a piece he called a *'Fantasie' Impromptu*, which again broadens the horizons of pianistic composition. By rights it should have been burnt according to Chopin's instructions. For whatever reason the composer was never happy with this work and it is fortunate for us that Chopin's student Julius Fontana sought to publish it and many other previously hidden works, like the *Largo in E flat major*.

In 1836 Chopin began an 11-year liaison, somewhat ambiguous in nature, with the novelist George Sand (real name Aurore Dudevant). She was a mother of two, separated from her husband, with striking looks and a reputation for intelligent, progressive thinking. In 1838 the couple went to the island of Majorca, but the damp conditions worsened Chopin's tuberculosis and they returned to France, staying in Sand's country home every summer until 1846. Sand was undoubtedly a huge inspiration to Chopin. His most deeply felt music comes from his years with her, and he wrote hardly anything after they parted. Without her nursing, Chopin's health quickly deteriorated and his professional life also began to falter. In 1848 his sister began to care for him, until he finally succumbed to the tuberculosis that had dogged him throughout his life in October 1849, at only 39 years of age.

Michael Ahmad, April 2007

Ballade No.1 in G minor
Op.23

Composed by Frédéric Chopin

Original key: G minor

Moderato

Barcarolle
Op.60

Composed by Frédéric Chopin

Original key: F♯ major

Allegretto

Berceuse
Op.57

Composed by Frédéric Chopin

Andante

Chorale from Nocturne
Op.37, No.1

Composed by Frédéric Chopin

Andante sostenuto

Étude No.3
Op.10

Composed by Frédéric Chopin

Original key: E major

'Fantaisie' Impromtu
Op.66, No.4

Composed by Frédéric Chopin

'Funeral March' from Sonata No.2
Op.35

Composed by Frédéric Chopin

Largo in E♭ major
Op. Posth.

Composed by Frédéric Chopin

Mazurka
Op.68, No.2

Composed by Frédéric Chopin

21

Mazurka
Op.7, No.5

Composed by Frédéric Chopin

Nocturne in E♭ major
Op.9, No.2

Composed by Frédéric Chopin

Andante

Mazurka
Op.67, No.2

Composed by Frédéric Chopin

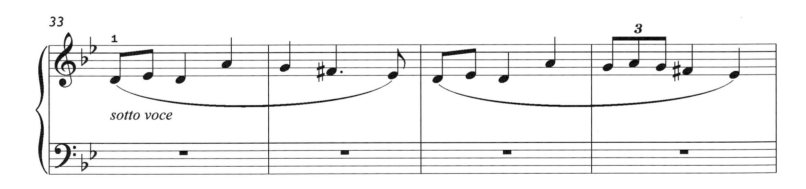

Ped. come sopra

Nocturne in G minor
Op.15, No.3

Composed by Frédéric Chopin

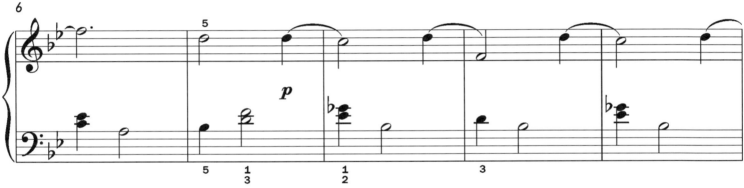

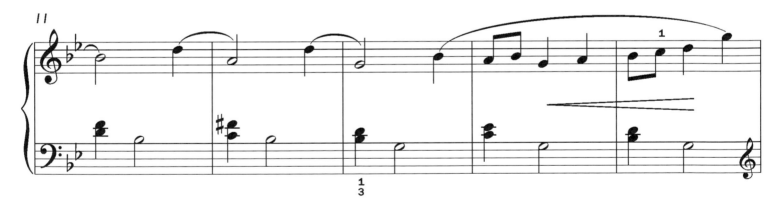

Piano Concerto No.1
Op.11 (2nd movement: Romance)

Composed by Frédéric Chopin

Original key: E major

33

Polonaise in A major 'Militaire'
Op.40, No.1

Composed by Frédéric Chopin

Original key: A major

Allegro con brio

poco rit.　　　　　**D.C. al Fine**

Polonaise
Op.53

Composed by Frédéric Chopin

Maestoso

Prélude in A major 'The Polish Dance'
Op.28, No.7

Composed by Frédéric Chopin

Prélude in C minor 'Funeral March'
Op.28, No.20

Composed by Frédéric Chopin

Prélude in B♭ major 'Sunday'
Op.28, No.21

Composed by Frédéric Chopin

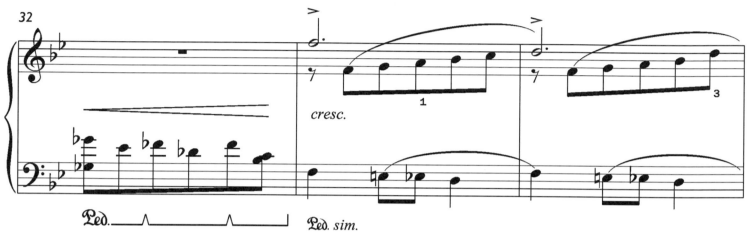

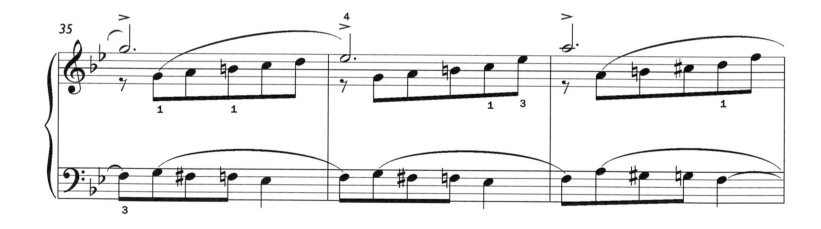

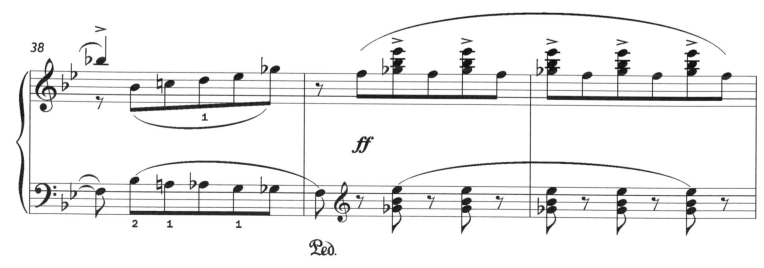

Prélude in D♭ major 'Raindrop'
Op.28, No.15

Composed by Frédéric Chopin

Sostenuto

Prelude in E minor 'Suffocation'
Op.28, No.4

Composed by Frédéric Chopin

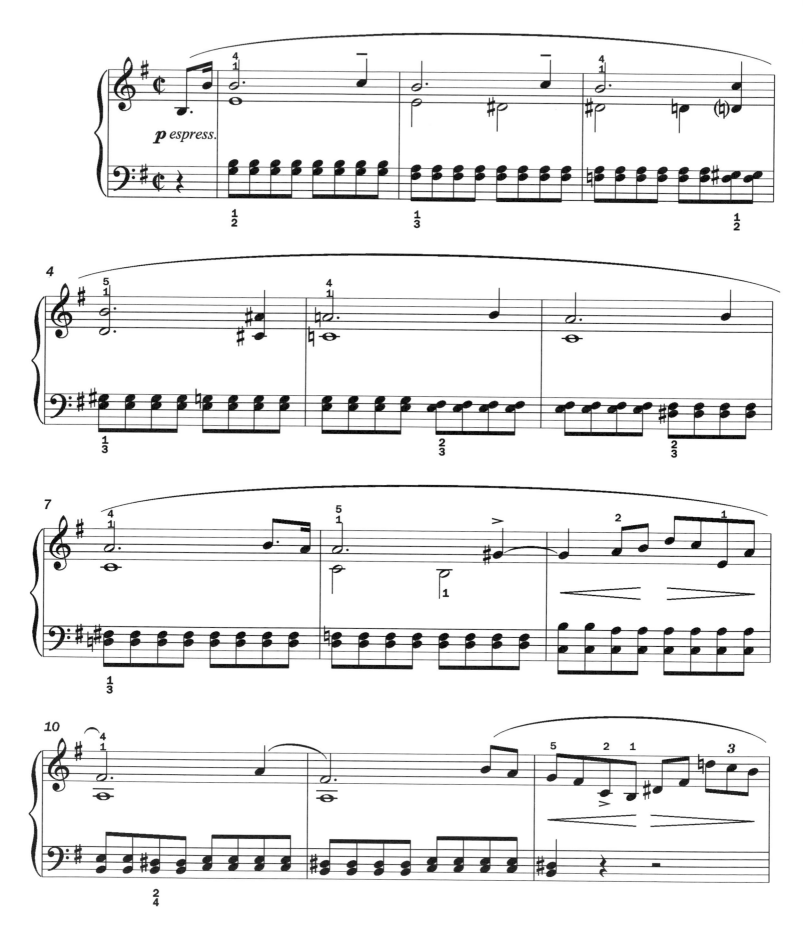

Sonata No.1 in C minor
Op.4 (2nd movement: Menuetto and Trio)

Composed by Frédéric Chopin

Original key: E♭ major

Menuetto

Allegretto

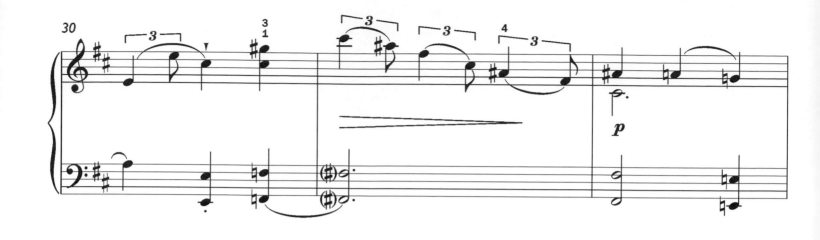

senza Ped.

Ped._____| Ped._____| *simile*

**Menuetto da Capo,
senza repetizione**

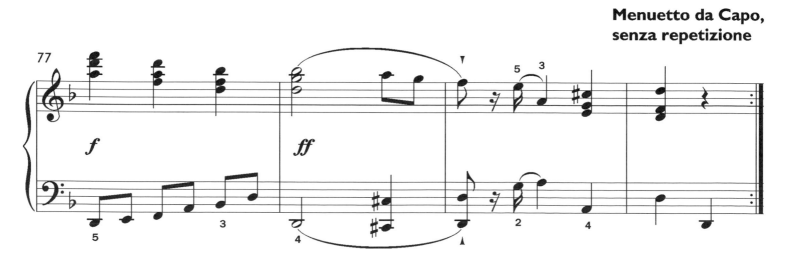

54

Waltz in A minor 'Brillante'
Op.34, No.2

Composed by Frédéric Chopin

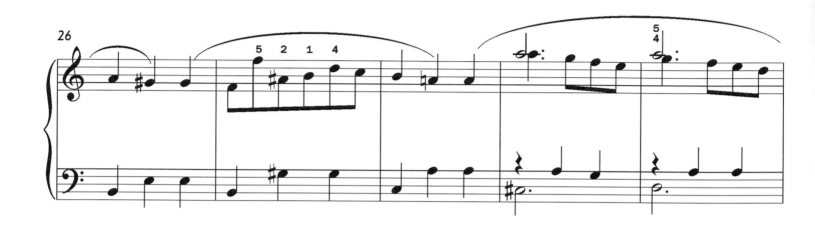

Sostenuto

Waltz in A♭ major 'Farewell' (Posthumous)
Op.69, No.1

Composed by Frédéric Chopin

Waltz in D♭ major 'Minute'
Op.64, No.1

Composed by Frédéric Chopin

Original key: D♭ major

Molto vivace

Cantabile in B♭ major

Composed by Frédéric Chopin